From Cuba to the United States

D0613318

by Maritza Lopez Garcia

NATIONAL GEOGRAPHIC LEARNING | CENGAGE

It is 90 miles from Florida to Cuba.

My name is Maritza. I am from Matanzas. It is a city in Cuba.

Now I live in Miami, Florida.

This is my family.
My mother—Maria Garcia de Lopez
My father—Ramon Lopez

Papi and Mateo
My brothers—Mateo Lopez Garcia; Luis Lopez Garcia
Luis is such a clown!

My aunt and uncle live in Miami.

Aunt Isabel Uncle Jorge

Their dog, Dante

They met us at the airport.

I miss my home in Cuba.

My home in Matanzas

The beach in Matanzas

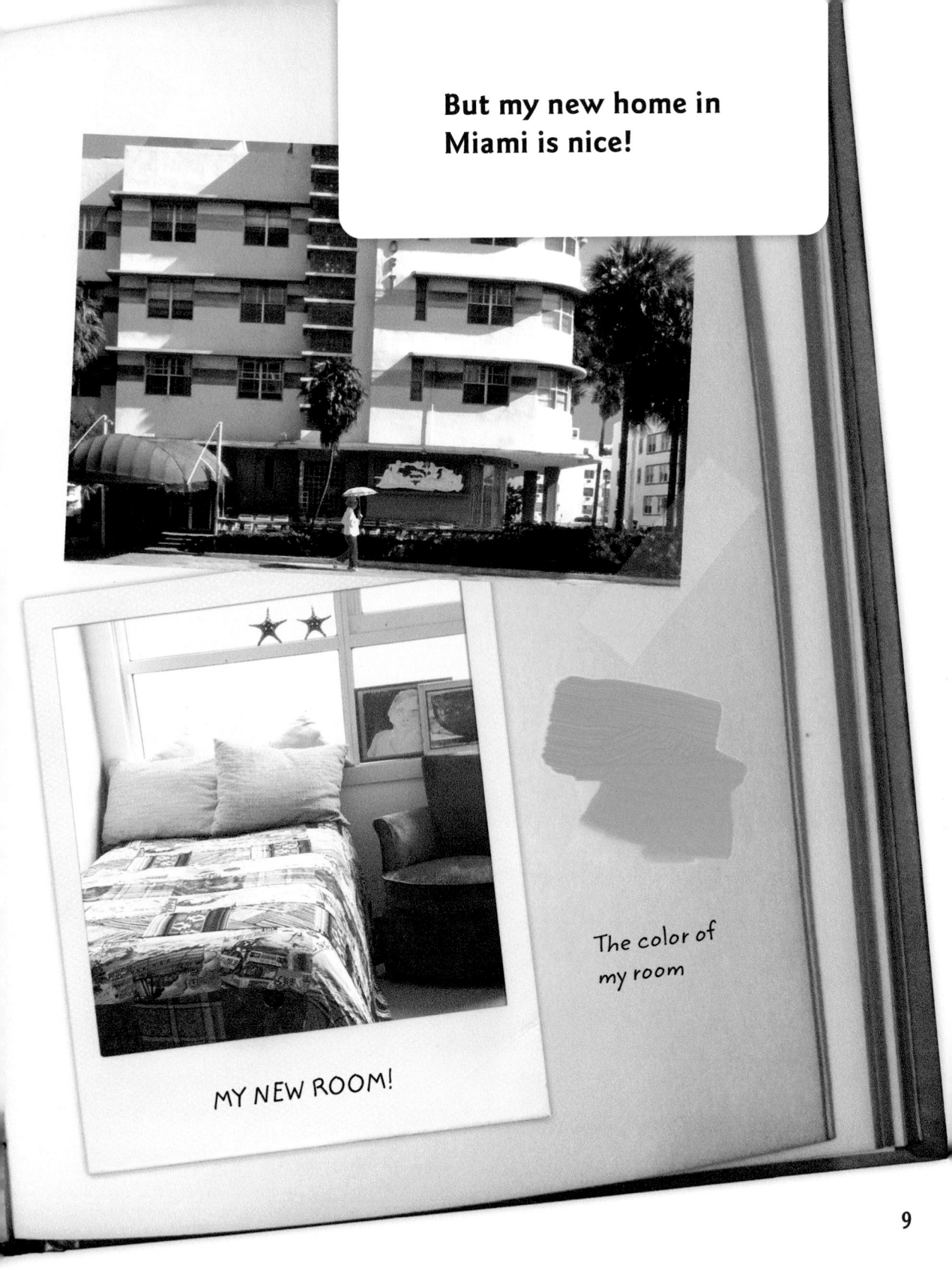
But my new home in Miami is nice!
MY NEW ROOM!
The color of my room

I have a lot of friends in Matanzas.

My friends in Cuba

Elena and Alicia

HECTOR!

A letter from Elena

¡Hola, Maritza!

¿Cómo te va? ¿Te gusta vivir en Miami? ¿Tienes muchos nuevos amigos?

Alicia y yo te extrañamos y pensamos mucho en ti. Aquí te envío una foto de nosotras dos.

Escríbenos pronto.

Elena

Now I have many friends in Miami!

My friends, Dalili and Andrea

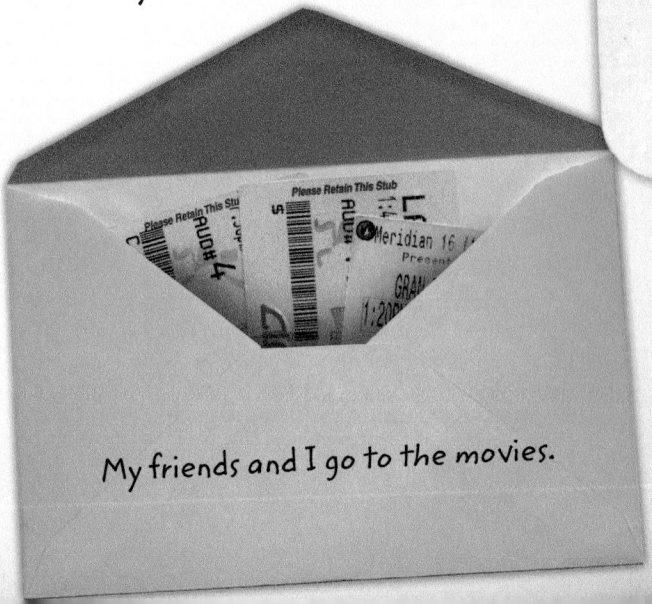

My friends and I go to the movies.

Friendship

We go to parties.
Happy Birthday
For : Carlos
Date : Saturday
Time : 5:00
Place : Andrea's House
R. S. V. P. 555-1234

Miami is a lot like Cuba.

Little Havana is a Cuban neighborhood in Miami.

People dance to salsa music at a street party.

I can find Cuban food here!

I LOVE good Cuban food.

The flag of Cuba

I miss Matanzas. But I like Miami, too!
MARITZA'S
SCRAPBOOK